TOP TENS

DEADLY
CREATURES

1 SEA WASP

2 PIRANHA

3 BEAKED SEA SNAKE

4 ANOPHELES MOSQUITO

5 FIERCE SNAKE

6 PALESTINE SCORPION

7 STONEFISH

8 BLUE RINGED OCTOPUS

9 SYDNEY FUNNEL WEB SPIDER

10 POISON DART FROG

Copyright © ticktock Entertainment Ltd 2005
First published in Great Britain in 2005 by ticktock Media Ltd,
Unit 2, Orchard Business Centre, North Farm Road, Tunbridge Wells, Kent TN2 3XF
ISBN 1 86007 911 3 pbk
Printed in China
A CIP catalogue record for this book is available from the British Library.

Picture credits (t=top; b=bottom; c=centre; l=left; r=right): Corbis: 6-7 all, 8-9 all. FLPA: 10-11 all, 12-13 all, 20-21 all,
22c, 24-25 all. Natural History Photo Library: 14-15 all, 16-17 all, 18-19 all, 23b, 26-27 all.

Every effort has been made to trace the copyright holders, and we apologise in advance for any
unintentional omissions. We would be pleased to insert the appropriate acknowledgements in any
subsequent edition of this publication.

CONTENTS

This book is a catalogue of the world's most deadly living creatures. There are lots and lots of dangerous animals around the world, and many of these can cause injury, and even death. But most of them are just dangerous because they are large or have sharp teeth. The creatures in this book are different – they are not just dangerous, they are killers one and all. Our top ten deadly creatures were rated according to:

SHAPE

When studying deadly creatures, it soon became clear that size was not particularly important. Instead, we gave points for complexity of shape – the animals with the most complex shapes were awarded the most points. A more complicated shape can make a creature difficult to recognize and avoid. Its shape may also give the creature an increased opportunity for attack.

NO.9 | SYDNEY FUNNEL-WEB SPIDER

The funnel-web spider that lives around the city of Sydney in Australia is probably the most dangerous spider on earth. Although it mainly lives in the woodland surrounding the city, the Sydney funnel-web spider is often found in garages and backyards, and even underneath the floors of houses.

SHAPE

The Sydney funnel-web is quite large for a spider, with a body length of about 2-4 centimetres. Males are more lightly built than females.

The Sydney funnel-web spider injects its venom through a pair of sharp, curved fangs.

DANGER

Most spiders have **venom** that is too weak to affect large animals. The Sydney funnel-web spider is unusual because its venom is super-deadly to human beings, and its **jaws** can bite through clothing.

ATTACK

This spider is an active hunter that wanders over the ground at night in search of **prey**. When threatened, it raises its head and forelegs before delivering its deadly bite.

8

DANGER

For this category we looked at all the features that make a particular animal dangerous, and gave them separate scores. We also considered whether the animal is aggressive (which increases its danger score), how widely it is distributed, and whether it is common or rare. The overall score is a combination of all these factors.

ATTACK

Here we examined the actual process of the animal's attack, and the mechanisms it uses to kill its victims. Animals that used an unusual method of attack were scored more highly than those that share their method of attack with many other creatures. Additional points were given to those deadly creatures that take their victims by surprise.

LETHAL

This category is only concerned with the physical effects of the venom, toxin or other substance that causes death. Wherever possible, records of attacks on human beings were examined, and the lethality of the substance expressed in terms of human deaths. The effects on any intended prey, which is generally much smaller than a human being, can be considered as the same.

PREY

Here, the focus is on what these deadly creatures eat – even if, as with the stonefish, they do not actually use their deadly characteristics while hunting. We looked at the size and variety of prey, and we also considered whether the prey was easy or difficult to locate.

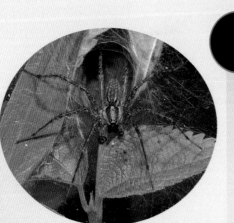

Funnel webs are dark brown in colour, and live in funnel-shaped retreats.

EXTREME SCORES

A spider with sharp fangs, deadly venom, and a reputation for being bad-tempered. Beware!

SHAPE

ATTACK

PREY

DANGER
LETHAL

= TOTAL SCORE

LETHAL
The Sydney funnel-web spider has its own unique venom. Once it gets into the bloodstream it begins to attack the **heart** and can cause death in less than one hour.

PREY
This spider will attack humans if it feels threatened, but it mainly eats snails, slugs and small **amphibians**, beetles, and cockroaches. They even eat small lizards.

POISON DART FROG

Most people think that small frogs are harmless, but the poison frog will soon make them change their minds. The poison frog lives in the tropical **rain forests** of Central and South America. Native people sometimes smear the frog's poison on the tips of their arrows and blowpipe darts when they go hunting.

SHAPE

The poison dart frog ranges in size from just over 2 centimetres (the Strawberry Poison Dart Frog) to 8 centimetres (Dyeing Poison Frog).

DANGER

This small **amphibian** uses poison as a defence mechanism. The bright colours warn **predators** that these frogs are definitely not good to eat.

ATTACK

A thin layer of deadly poisonous slime covers the poison dart frog. The slime oozes from small **glands** in the frog's skin.

The frog's bright colouration is a vivid warning: do not touch!

LETHAL

The glands produce a **toxin** that stops muscles from working and causes death. Just touching a poison frog can transfer enough toxin to kill an adult human being.

PREY

The poison dart frog mainly feeds on insects; especially ants, which it needs to eat in order to produce its toxin.

The skin of the poison dart frog is coated with poisonous slime.

This frog is small, attractive and deadly. If you see one, do not be tempted to touch it.

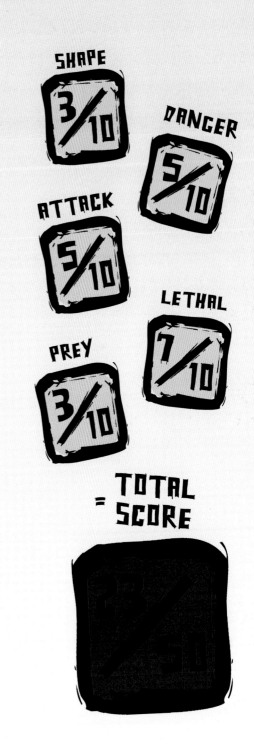

SHAPE
3/10

DANGER
5/10

ATTACK
5/10

LETHAL
7/10

PREY
3/10

= TOTAL SCORE

The funnel-web spider that lives around the city of Sydney in Australia is probably the most dangerous spider on earth. Although it mainly lives in the woodland surrounding the city, the Sydney funnel-web spider is often found in garages and backyards, and even underneath the floors of houses.

SHAPE

The Sydney funnel-web is quite large for a spider, with a body length of about 2-4 centimetres. Males are more lightly built than females.

The Sydney funnel-web spider injects its venom through a pair of sharp, curved **fangs.**

DANGER

Most spiders have **venom** that is too weak to affect large animals. The Sydney funnel-web spider is unusual because its venom is super-deadly to human beings, and its **jaws** can bite through clothing.

ATTACK

This spider is an active hunter that wanders over the ground at night in search of **prey**. When threatened, it raises its head and forelegs before delivering its deadly bite.

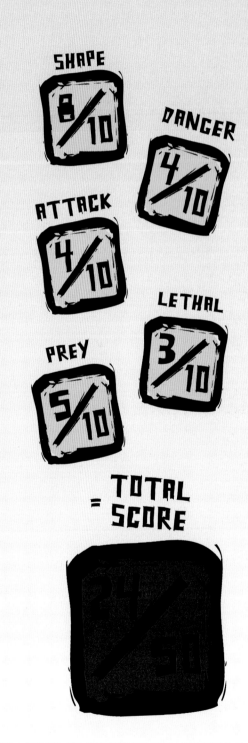

Funnel webs are dark brown in colour, and live in funnel-shaped retreats.

A spider with sharp fangs, deadly venom, and a reputation for being bad-tempered. Beware!

SHAPE
8/10

DANGER
4/10

ATTACK
4/10

LETHAL
3/10

PREY
5/10

= TOTAL SCORE

LETHAL

The Sydney funnel-web spider has its own unique venom. Once it gets into the bloodstream it begins to attack the **heart** and can cause death in less than one hour.

PREY

This spider will attack humans if it feels threatened, but it mainly eats snails, slugs and small **amphibians**, beetles, and cockroaches. They even eat small lizards.

The blue-ringed octopus is one of the most beautiful of all sea creatures – it is also one of the most deadly. This small, shy animal lives around coral reefs in the Indian and Pacific oceans. Swimmers and divers have learned not to go looking for this octopus because it has a very nasty bite.

SHAPE

Like all octopi, this one has a soft body with eight arms. The blue-ringed octopus is only about 10 centimetres long – about the size of a golf ball.

DANGER

The blue-ringed octopus is the only octopus that has a **venomous** bite. People swimming in the sea that accidentally disturb this octopus are likely to get bitten with lethal results.

ATTACK

The octopus has a sharp beak that can slice into flesh. This allows its venomous **saliva** to flow into the wound.

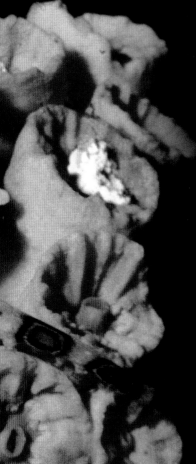

A blue-ringed octopus weighs
about 30 grams.

LETHAL

At first the bite feels like a bee-sting. Then the victim goes numb and dies. There is no known **antidote** for blue-ringed octopus **venom**.

PREY

This octopus feeds mainly on crabs, and wounded fish that cannot swim away quickly.

The blue rings are a warning that the octopus is angry or frightened – in either case it may bite.

A beautiful but deadly animal that is active during the day, which is when most people go swimming – make sure you take care in the water!

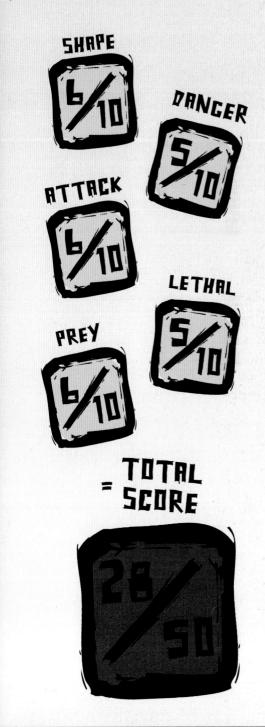

SHAPE 6/10

DANGER 5/10

ATTACK 6/10

LETHAL 5/10

PREY 6/10

= TOTAL SCORE 28/50

STONEFISH

Meet the fish that looks just like a rock – the stonefish, which lives around the coasts of the Indian and Pacific oceans. Not only is it very ugly, it is also very dangerous, because the stonefish is the most **venomous** fish in the sea. Its sharp spines can easily penetrate flesh and inject their deadly venom.

SHAPE

A stonefish can grow up to 50 centimetres in length, with lumpy skin as **camouflage** that helps disguise its shape.

DANGER

The stonefish likes to lie half buried on the seabed waiting in ambush for its **prey**. People paddling or swimming in the sea sometimes step on a camouflaged stonefish by mistake.

A stonefish does not swim away when disturbed, it turns to face the intruder.

ATTACK

There are 13 sharp, hollow spines in the fin running along the stonefish's back. Each of these spines can inject a deadly dose of venom.

LETHAL

If you step on a stonefish it will start to hurt straight away, and the pain will rapidly get worse. Some victims die within a few hours.

PREY

The stonefish only uses its spines for defence. It waits for shrimp and small fish to pass by, then strikes, gulping them down in under a second.

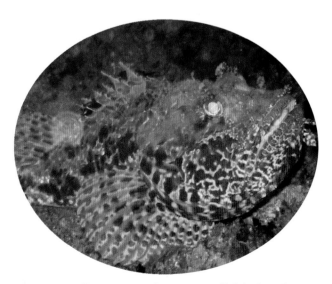

The fin along the stonefish's back contains no less than 13 nasty surprises.

Spines full of deadly venom hidden on a camouflaged fish – make sure that the next stone you step on really is a stone and not a stonefish.

SHAPE 5/10

DANGER 7/10

ATTACK 7/10

LETHAL 5/10

PREY 5/10

= TOTAL SCORE

The Palestine scorpion is the most dangerous scorpion in the world. It is found in the **deserts** and scrubland of the Middle East and North Africa. The Palestine scorpion is so deadly that local people have given it the name "Deathstalker".

SHAPE

The Palestine Scorpion is about 8-11 centimetres long with two large **pincers** and a deadly tail **sting**.

DANGER

This monster often hides under rocks or among loose sand and stones. If disturbed it will lash out with its deadly tail. Children are often stung while playing or walking to and from school.

ATTACK

The sharp sting penetrates flesh and injects deadly venom. The Palestine scorpion will sometimes sting a victim over and over again.

The sting at the end the Deathstalker's curving tail carries a load of deadly venom.

Yellow coloration helps the scorpion to hide in desert sand.

LETHAL

One drop of the venom is enough to kill an animal much larger than itself. Fortunately, scientists have developed an **antidote** for the sting of the Palestine scorpion.

PREY

It hunts insects but does not use its sting; instead it tears its **prey** apart with its pincers.

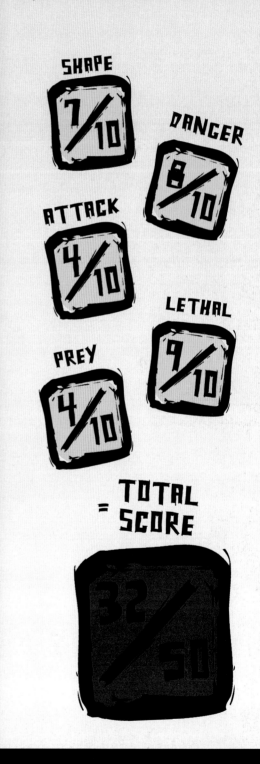

The Palestine scorpion lives up to its nickname - "Deathstalker" — so stay away from the desert.

SHAPE
7/10

DANGER
8/10

ATTACK
4/10

LETHAL
9/10

PREY
4/10

= TOTAL SCORE

33/50

FIERCE SNAKE

The Fierce Snake is not as famous as cobras and rattlesnakes, but it is a lot more deadly because it has the deadliest venom of any snake. The fierce snake, which is also known as the "inland taipan", is only found in central and northern Australia where it is very rare. The first live specimen was not captured until 1975.

SHAPE

The Fierce Snake grows up to 2.5 metres long. Its smooth body is brown in colour with a mustard yellow belly and a glossy black head.

The fierce snake has enough deadly venom to kill 100 people.

DANGER

The fierce snake is shy and rare and usually docile, but if you are unlucky enough to see one – walk slowly away, because it can be very aggressive if disturbed.

ATTACK

This snake can strike faster than the eye can follow. As it bites its victim, two hollow **fangs** inject a small dose of its venom.

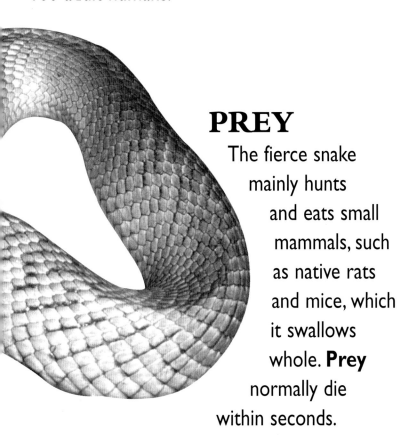

Inside the mouth are two sharp
fangs that inject venom into victims.

LETHAL

This creature has the most toxic venom of
any snake. The fierce snake carries enough
poison to kill about 250,000 mice, or about
100 adult humans.

PREY

The fierce snake
mainly hunts
and eats small
mammals, such
as native rats
and mice, which
it swallows
whole. **Prey**
normally die
within seconds.

How can you rate the world's
deadliest snake? Fortunately for us, the
fierce snake is very rare.

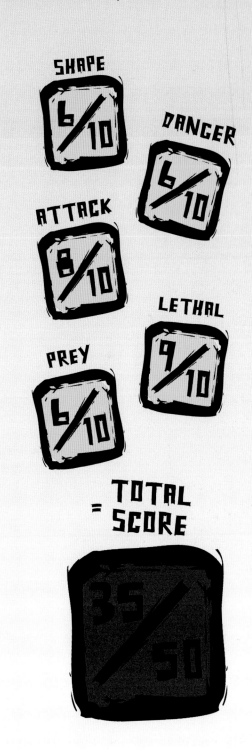

SHAPE 6/10

DANGER 6/10

ATTACK 8/10

LETHAL 9/10

PREY 6/10

= TOTAL SCORE

35/50

ANOPHELES MOSQUITO

"Mosquito" is a Portuguese word meaning little fly, and its use dates back to about 1583. The mosquito just wants to drink a little warm, human blood. But while it drinks our blood, the anopheles mosquito also gives us the deadly disease called **malaria**, and has killed more people than any other animal on our planet.

SHAPE

A mosquito has two scaled wings, a slender body, and six long legs. They can vary in size but are rarely larger than 15 millimetres.

DANGER

The anopheles mosquito has a tiny **microbe** living in its body. When it sucks blood, the microbe leaks into the victim's bloodstream. In human victims, this microbe causes the killer disease malaria.

ATTACK

A mosquito does not bite with teeth. It has a feeding tube like a hollow needle. It jabs this tube into human skin to suck up blood.

Female mosquitoes must drink blood in order to lay eggs.

LETHAL

Taking a tiny amount of blood causes no problem at all. But **malaria** has killed hundreds of millions of people throughout human history.

Each mosquito takes just a tiny drop of bright red blood.

PREY

Mosquitoes are only interested in drinking the blood of **mammals** – humans are easy targets but mosquito adults also feed on flower nectar and juices of fruits for flight energy.

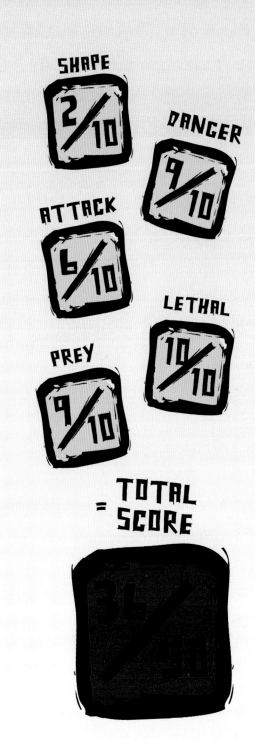

Small and hard to see, the anopheles does not look like a killer, but it has caused untold millions of human deaths.

SHAPE
2/10

DANGER
9/10

ATTACK
6/10

LETHAL
10/10

PREY
9/10

= TOTAL SCORE

BEAKED SEA SNAKE

The **Beaked sea snake** lives in the Pacific Ocean area around Australia. This sea snake is a bad-tempered killer. This one **species** is responsible for about half of all sea snake attacks, and for 90 percent of deaths from sea snake bites. The venom of the beaked sea snake is deadlier than that of most land snakes.

SHAPE

This snake can reach a length of up to 2 metres. They have specialized flattened tails for swimming and veils over their nostrils which are closed in water.

DANGER

The beaked sea snake is often caught in fishing nets. People trying to take the snakes out of the nets are the ones most likely to get bitten. The beaked sea snake is responsible for more than half of all cases of sea snake bites.

Vivid black markings make this deadly sea snake easy to identify.

ATTACK

Sea snakes have much shorter **fangs** than land snakes – just 2-4 millimetres long but they are just as sharp and deadly. The venom of the beaked sea snake acts very quickly.

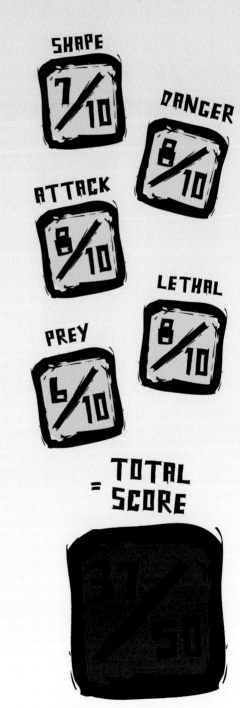

The beaked sea snake grows
to about 1.3 metres long.

An aggressive and bad-tempered
animal with sharp fangs and deadly
venom – the beaked sea snake would
certainly not make a good pet.

SHAPE
7/10

DANGER
8/10

ATTACK
8/10

LETHAL
8/10

PREY
6/10

= TOTAL SCORE
37/50

LETHAL

The venom is the sixth most deadly
of any snake in the world. It attacks the
muscles and stops the victim from breathing,
which quickly causes death. Just one drop of
venom is enough to kill three men.

PREY

The beaked sea snake can swallow its **prey**
twice the size of its neck. This strange
snake's main diet is fish, fish eggs and eels.

PIRANHA

This fish has earned its nickname of the "Wolf of the Waters". It has sharp teeth and hunts in groups – one piranha will give you a nasty bite, but a group of them will strip all the flesh from your bones. The piranha is found in the Amazon and other rivers in South America.

SHAPE

The average length is about 30 centimetres, but a well-fed piranha can reach twicethat size.

When piranhas are in a feeding frenzy, the water seems to churn and turns red with blood.

DANGER

The piranha has a superb sense of smell and can detect blood in the water from more than a mile away. It lives in **shoals** of 100 or so fish that can all attack at the same time.

ATTACK

Piranhas do not kill their prey, they just start eating it alive! Their teeth are triangular in shape and are razor sharp. When they have finished feeding, only the bones are left.

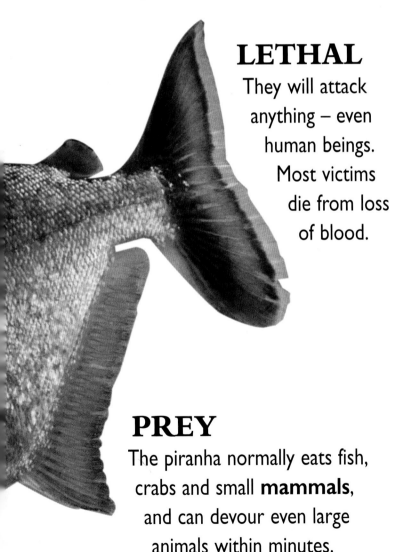

The teeth of the piranha are specialised flesh slicers.

LETHAL

They will attack anything – even human beings. Most victims die from loss of blood.

PREY

The piranha normally eats fish, crabs and small **mammals**, and can devour even large animals within minutes.

EXTREME SCORES

The flesh-eating piranha makes another good reason to stay out of the water – this fish will start eating unwary swimmers without any warning.

SHAPE
4/10

DANGER
9/10

ATTACK
10/10

LETHAL
7/10

PREY
10/10

= TOTAL SCORE
/50

SEA WASP

The final verdict – no living creature is more deadly than this jellyfish. This small, boneless animal is found in the seas around Australia. It has dozens of **stinging tentacles** armed with deadly venom that kills almost instantly. To make matters worse, the transparent and colourless sea wasp is almost impossible to see underwater.

SHAPE

It has a roughly four-sided shape (it is also known as the box jelly) and grows to about 30 centimetres in width, with tentacles that are more than 100 centimetres in length.

All jellyfish have a soft, hollow body.

DANGER

Hundreds of people are stung every year, and many die. To protect people, many beaches in Australia are closed when there are sea wasps about.

PREY

The sea wasp feeds mainly on shrimp and small fish.

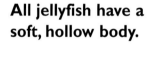

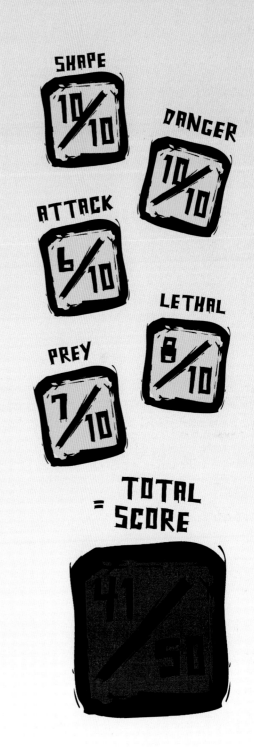

The white blobs on the tentacles are clusters of tiny, spring-loaded stings.

ATTACK

Every tentacle has thousands of tiny, coiled stings, each one with a sharp point. These stings are triggered by the slightest touch and inject deadly venom into the victim.

LETHAL

Sea wasp victims feel a sudden burning pain, and the venom may stop the **heart** from beating within a few minutes. A single sea wasp carries enough venom to kill about 50 human beings.

Not just deadly, this creature is almost impossible to see, which is more than enough reason to avoid it at all costs!

SHAPE
10/10

DANGER
10/10

ATTACK
6/10

LETHAL
8/10

PREY
7/10

= TOTAL SCORE

41/50

Before deciding our Top Ten Deadly Creatures, we also considered these animals – all of them are deadly killers, but not quite deadly enough to make the Top Ten.

CONE SHELL

The cone shell is a kind of marine gastropod (sea snail). Its shell is about 7-10 centimetres long, and it is often brightly coloured. If you saw one on a beach, you might be tempted to pick it up – bad move! All cone shells can inflict a painful sting, and some **species** also inject a deadly **toxin**.

GILA MONSTER

This strange-looking reptile is one of only two venomous lizards in the whole world – and they both live in the **deserts** of the southwestern United States of America, and northern Mexico. The gila monster does not have two long **fangs** to injects its venom, like poisonous snakes. It has short teeth, but they are all venomous, and the venom is strong enough to kill an adult human.

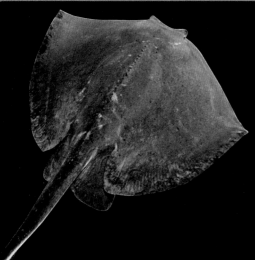

STINGRAY

The stingray is closely related to sharks, but you do not have to worry about its bite – it's the sting in the tail that's the problem. This fish likes shallow water, and often hides in the sand on the seabed. Unwary swimmers and paddlers are liable to be speared by the long, venomous spine that is located near the base of the stingray's long tail.

HARVESTER ANT

Harvester ants are common in the United States of America. They like to collect plant seeds without any disturbance. If any human beings get in their way – maybe while having a picnic – then the humans had better watch out! Harvester ants are equipped with a sharp **sting** that injects dangerous venom. Pain and itching are immediate, and death sometimes follows.

WESTERN DIAMOND BACK RATTLESNAKE

The western diamond-back is the strongest and most aggressive of the North American rattlesnakes. This highly dangerous snake prefers to keep its venom for **prey** that is small enough for it to swallow. Large intruders are warned by the distinctive rattle, and they had better beware – this killer bites fast and bites deep.

NO. 10 POISON DART FROG

Animal type	Amphibian	Extreme Scores	
Location	Central and South America	Shape	3
Size	2-6cm	Danger	5
Diet	Mainly insects	Attack	5
Habitat	Rainforest	Lethal	7
Notable feature	Poisonous skin	Prey	3

TOTAL SCORE 23/50

NO. 9 SYDNEY FUNNEL-WEB SPIDER

Animal type	Arachnid	Extreme Scores	
Location	Australia	Shape	8
Size	2-4cm	Danger	4
Diet	Insects, amphibians, etc.	Attack	4
Habitat	Mostly woodland	Lethal	3
Notable feature	Deadly venom	Prey	5

TOTAL SCORE 24/50

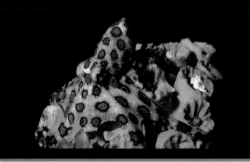

NO. 8 BLUE-RINGED OCTOPUS

Animal type	Cephalopod	Extreme Scores	
Location	Indo-Pacific	Shape	6
Size	10cm	Danger	5
Diet	Crabs and fish	Attack	6
Habitat	Indian and Pacific ocean	Lethal	5
Notable feature	Deadly saliva	Prey	6

TOTAL SCORE 28/50

NO. 7 STONEFISH

Animal type	Bony fish	Extreme Scores	
Location	Indo-Pacific	Shape	5
Size	60cm	Danger	7
Diet	Shrimps and small fish	Attack	7
Habitat	Indian and Pacific ocean	Lethal	5
Notable feature	Deadly spines	Prey	5

TOTAL SCORE 29/50

NO. 6 PALESTINE SCORPION

Animal type	Arachnid	Extreme Scores	
Location	Middle East	Shape	7
Size	8-11cm	Danger	8
Diet	Insects	Attack	4
Habitat	Deserts and scrubland	Lethal	9
Notable feature	Deadly sting	Prey	4

TOTAL SCORE 32/50

NO. 5 FIERCE SNAKE

Animal type	Reptile	**Extreme Scores**	**TOTAL SCORE**
Location	Australia	Shape	6
Size	2.5m	Danger	6
Diet	Small mammals	Attack	8
Habitat	Forests and plains	Lethal	9
Notable feature	Deadly venom	Prey	6

35 / 50

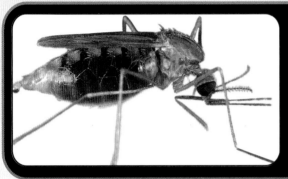

NO. 4 ANOPHELES MOSQUITO

Animal type	Insect	**Extreme Scores**	**TOTAL SCORE**
Location	Worldwide	Shape	2
Size	8mm	Danger	9
Diet	Mammal blood	Attack	6
Habitat	Around water	Lethal	10
Notable feature	Transmits disease	Prey	9

36 / 50

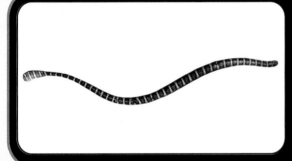

NO. 3 BEAKED SEA SNAKE

Animal type	Reptile	**Extreme Scores**	**TOTAL SCORE**
Location	Indo-Pacific	Shape	7
Size	2m	Danger	8
Diet	Fish, fish eggs and eels	Attack	8
Habitat	Pacific Ocean	Lethal	8
Notable feature	Deadly venom	Prey	6

37 / 50

NO. 2 PIRANHA

Animal type	Bony fish	**Extreme Scores**	**TOTAL SCORE**
Location	South America	Shape	4
Size	30-60cm	Danger	9
Diet	Fish, crabs and mammals	Attack	10
Habitat	Rivers	Lethal	7
Notable feature	Razor sharp teeth	Prey	10

40 / 50

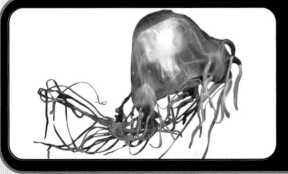

NO. 1 SEA WASP

Animal type	Cnidarian	**Extreme Scores**	**TOTAL SCORE**
Location	Indo-Pacific	Shape	10
Size	30cm	Danger	10
Diet	Shrimp and small fish	Attack	6
Habitat	Rivers around Australia	Lethal	8
Notable feature	Stinging tentacles	Prey	7

41 / 50

GLOSSARY

AMPHIBIAN an animal capable of living both on land and in water

ANTIDOTE a remedy used to neutralize or counteract the effects of a poison

CAMOUFLAGE means of of disguise by protective colouring or shape

CORAL REEF a reef consisting of coral – the external skeleton of a group of marine animals

DESERT waterless area of land with little or no vegetation

FANG a hollow tooth of a venomous snake with which it injects its poison, or a canine tooth of a carnivorous animal with which it seizes and tears its prey

GLAND organ of the body which secretes chemical substances

HEART organ that pumps blood through the circulatory system

JAWS the structures that form the framework of the mouth and hold the teeth

MALARIA infectious disease characterized by cycles of chills, fever, and sweating transmitted to humans by the bite of an infected female anopheles mosquito

MAMMAL any of various warm-blooded animals with a covering of hair on the skin and, in the female, the ability to produce milk with which to feed the young

MICROBE a minute life form; a micro-organism, especially a bacterium that causes disease

PINCERS front claw of a lobster, crab, or similar creature

PREDATOR an animal that lives by preying on other animals

PREY an animal hunted or caught for food

RAIN FOREST a dense evergreen forest occupying a tropical region with an annual rainfall of at least 2.5 metres

SALIVA watery liquid secreted into the mouth by glands

SHOAL a large group of fish or other marine animals

SPECIES a class of individuals or objects grouped by virtue of their common attributes and assigned a common name

STING a sharp, piercing organ or part, often ejecting a venomous secretion

TENTACLE a flexible organ near the head mouth in many animals used for feeling or grasping

TOXIN a poisonous substance that is produced by living cells or organisms capable of causing disease when introduced into the body

VENOM a poisonous secretion of an animal, such as a snake, spider, or scorpion, usually transmitted by a bite or sting

VENOMOUS a creature that can produce venom

INDEX

A
Amphibian 28, 30
Anopheles mosquito
   18-19, 29, 30
antidote 30
Arachnids 28
attack score 5

B
Beaked sea snake
   20-21, 29
Blue-ringed octopus
   10-11, 28
bony fish 28, 29

C
camouflage 30
Cephalopod 28
Cnidarian 29
Cone shell 26
coral reef 30

D
danger score 5
"Deathstalker" 14
desert 30

E
extreme scores 4-5

F
fang 30
Fierce snake 16-17, 29
fish 12-13, 22-23, 27-29
frogs see Poison
   dart frog
funnel-web spider
   8-9, 28

G
Gila monster 26
gland 30

H
Harvester ant 27
heart 30

I
inland taipan see Fierce snake
insects 27, 29

J
jaws 30
jellyfish see Sea wasp

L
lethal score 5
lizards see Gila monster

M
malaria 18-19, 30
mammal 30
microbe 31
mosquito see
   Anopheles mosquito

O
octopus see
   Blue-ringed octopus

P
Palestine scorpion
   14-15, 28
pincers 31
Piranha 22-23, 29
Pogonomyrmex 27
Poison dart frog 6-7, 28

predator 31
prey 31
prey score 5

R
rain forest 31
rattlesnake 27
reptiles 26, 29

S
saliva 31
scorpion see
      Palestine scorpion
Sea snail 26
Sea wasp 24-25, 29
shape score 4
shoal 31
snakes 16-17, 20-21, 29
species 31
spiders 8-9
sting 31
Stingray 27
Stonefish 12-13, 28
Sydney funnel
      web spider 8-9, 28

T
tentacle 31
toxin 31

V
venom 31
venomous 31

W
Western diamond-back
      rattlesnake 27
"Wolf of the Waters" 22